BECOME A MONEY MAGNET
The Real Investing Guide for People Who are Tired of Being Broke

BECOME A MONEY MAGNET
The Real Investing Guide for People Who are Tired of Being Broke

Raymond Sharp, M.Ed.

Copyright: 2017

All Rights Reserved

Printed in the United States of America

ISBN: 978-0-9890167-2-8

BOOK RAYMOND SHARP FOR AN IN-DEPTH REAL ESTATE WORKSHOP OR SEMINAR. SEND YOUR REQUEST TO SHARPSEMINARS@GMAIL.COM.

THIS BOOK IS DEDICATED TO EVERYONE WHO IS TIRED
OF STRUGGLING
AND CARES ENOUGH TO DO SOMETHING ABOUT IT.

CONTENTS

INTRODUCTION

ONE: Busting the Myths...1

TWO: Beginning Steps: Starting From Scratch....................................7

THREE: Developing Your Real Estate Investing Strategy.................17

FOUR: Residential Investing Basics..28

FIVE: Land Investing Basics...38

SIX: Commercial Investing Basics..42

APPENDIX A: Economic Development through Real Estate...........48

APPENDIX B: Tips for Negotiating..52

APPENDIX C: Mining for Diamonds: Finding the Next Deal..........57

APPENDIX D: Common Real Estate Terms and Definitions.......... 65

INTRODUCTION

I am passionate about real estate investing because it has made a tremendous impact on my life. I witnessed my parents work hard for their entire lives. My father served for over 20 years in the Army, and my mother held many part-time jobs until she landed a position with the United States Postal Service. Growing up, I held the belief that one must attend college and obtain a good job in order to have financial success in life. I also thought hard work would guarantee raises and promotions. Upon graduating from college, embarking on a career as an educator, and starting a family, I realized the time I spent at work did not measure the compensation I was receiving. I went on to receive a master's degree, but it did not influence my income. I learned a valuable lesson: I needed to find ways to make money that did not place limitations on my time or my earning potential.

One day, I was presented with an opportunity to pursue real estate as an agent. I jumped at the opportunity because I wanted to do something in the evenings and on weekends to supplement my income without interfering with my career. While learning about real estate investing, I discovered that many people were also in my predicament: college graduates with careers who were living paycheck to paycheck, experiencing the sad reality of ends not meeting. The conversations grew worse, especially as the economy turned downward. Many of my peers were no longer getting raises, and others were getting laid off. As I learned and gained knowledge about investing, I shared it with anyone who needed help and would listen.

One of the best lessons I learned from working with real estate investors during the recession was that the downturn prompted their property acquisition rate to increase between 35 and 60 percent, compared to years when the country was doing well financially. I learned that a savvy real estate investor will always find a way to take advantage of any market and financial situation. In other words, there is never a bad time to find a good real estate investment.

After learning lessons from homebuyers, business owners, and investors, I went on to start my own real estate and property management companies, and to educate others about real estate. Education is my passion, and will always be a part of my life. I have used my experience as an educator to explain the basics of real estate to make this easy for others to understand and apply. I am not an individual who only has ideas; I personally use the principles that I teach and share.

I understand that the fear of the unknown is a barrier that stops many people from moving forward in real estate investing. In fact, it was once a barrier for me. Overcoming this fear is one of the reasons I am writing this book. I want people to get so comfortable with investing in real estate that it becomes as easy as deciding what to wear for the day. In order to get dressed, a person needs to determine which clothes are currently available to wear, the expectation for his/her appearance, the predicted weather conditions, and how his/her circumstances may change throughout the day. Real estate investing is no different. One must analyze a property, determine its conditions, and question its financial potential in a particular market. A real estate investor must recognize patterns, and how the market may change in upcoming years. Real estate investors must also determine their options, as decisions must be made based regarding components such as minor repairs and major renovations, and the potential financial impact they may have.

I will go through these steps in a way that will give you comfort, confidence, and more money in your pocket. As an educator and a realtor, I see it as an obligation to make certain that you are prepared, and can make decisions with confidence. Fear will no longer be a barrier. Think of this book as a cheat sheet. Once you understand the principles and your options, nothing can stop you.

Even if your story is not my story, I believe everyone can benefit from making more money to support a family, prepare for retirement, or just to enjoy a better quality of life. Just to make things practical, let me ask you a question: What impact would an extra $2,500 a month have on your budget? It may sound like a drop in the bucket for people who want to become millionaires, but this is where it begins. I know people who supplement their income by earning anywhere from an extra $800 to $15,000 a month through real estate investments. I have worked people from all walks of life, such as business owners, college students, and employees at non-profit organizations, government entities, and even part-time and unemployed individuals who have taken advantage of real estate deals that have added value to their lives. I want you to understand this fact: real estate investing is for everyone. Real estate investing may not be your career, but it can be a very useful tool to provide a better life for you and your family. As the saying goes, a builder is only as good as his tools. If you want to improve your finances, there is no greater tool than real estate. Take advantage of this opportunity to gain valuable insights about using real estate investing as a wealth buildering tool.

I conduct my business with these core principles:

1. Find clients the best possible properties for the best possible price.
2. Educate clients so they are comfortable and trust the decisions they are making.
3. Leave clients in an equity positon to sell or lease their property.

Although the strategies I share can be applied to any real estate deal, every transaction is different. As the laws that govern processes can vary state to state, I always advise real estate investors to enlist the expertise of a licensed realtor. Make sure this person is active in the business, as you may encounter a former realtor who is out of the loop when it comes to current rules and regulations. From a realtor standpoint, rules, forms, and requirements change from year to year. As a consumer on the cusp of making a several hundred-thousand-dollar transaction, you want be sure that you have the most up-to-date information from a licensed professional.

This book will go over basic and intermediate strategizes and tools to invest in residential, commercial, and land transactions. This book also contains four appendix sections that serve as opportunists to develop your strategies and the basics of real estate. The appendices tackle negotiating, creating opportunities for economic development in your local community, finding opportunities, and common real estate terms.

This book is a beginning point to get you started in the right direction. I know this book will provoke though, and sound principles while giving a perspective that can make the difference between earning a few thousand dollars and hundreds of thousands of dollars.

Chapter 1
BUSTING THE MYTHS

Investing in real estate has developed a negative reputation due to the financial crisis and recession of 2008. During the recession, phrases that were once obscure became well known. Terms such as "underwater," "short sale," "foreclosure," and "toxic loans" became household words that too many people had to consider. However, a true real estate investor will learn how to turn a negative situation into a financial gain many times over. I am going to make my next statement with full confidence and experience backing me: real estate is always a good investment. Real estate investing runs in cycles; once an investor understands how to take advantage of the ebbs and flows of their market, he/she will be in a position for financial success.

One mistake the media makes is painting real estate with a broad brush. Real estate is a local and regional phenomenon. For example, areas surrounding military instillations did not suffer as much as other markets during the financial downturn in 2008. Furthermore, as the banks raised qualifications limits for loans, first-time home buyers were less able to purchase properties. Therefore, savvy real estate investors knew to focus more on renters during this time, since banks were not lending to buyers.

With real estate, there is always a silver lining and a way to make money. Unfortunately, one of the catalysts of the 2008 recession of resulted from banks giving mortgage loans to individuals who were not prepared to handle mortgage payments. Real estate markets in Georgia and Florida gravely suffered due to mortgage fraud that took advantage of consumers by overvaluing property. I mention these events because they are isolated, as these incidents are disgusting and have no place among most real estate professionals. Yes, they were widely reported, but they do not speak to the overall picture of real estate in the United States.

Real estate is strong, viable, relatable, and profitable. One must take time to avoid the noise to see the truth: real estate is a gateway to prosperity. There are many well-known individuals who have parlayed real estate into tremendous wealth, but furthermore, there are countless more men and women who, although they are not well known, also have the potential to succeed in real estate investing.

I want to take time to press "reset" on many of the negative things that discourage individuals from investing in real estate. There are many ways to make money in real estate, and it does not stop with residential homes. There are opportunities in land and commercial real estate, as well. This book will identify some of the common ways and some lesser-known methods to profitability. In the end, do not listen to the noise of those who are afraid to try something different. Real estate investing is more about thinking about creating solutions than it is about picking out a paint color. Real estate investors create solutions for society every day by creating access to dreams at home and in business. Collaboratively, real estate investors are on the pulse of the needs of their communities, working as innovators who think wisely and profit from what they know. If you are willing to humor me, this quick guide for success in real estate investing will help shift your perspective to the opportunities you walk past every single day. Especially in regards to land, shifting and expanding your horizons will help you build a stronger sense of community while increasing your bottom line.

I want to take a moment to speak to potential investors who feel they do not have enough money or a credit score that is worthy of becoming a real estate investor. Numerous individuals and financial institutions are using creative methods to help people finance property every day. There are better tools to help consider the investment and its profitability, beyond more than a particular individual's credit missteps along the way. You should not allow your current financial situation to deter you from seeking an opportunity to invest in real estate. Now, more than ever, realtors and financial institutions are working together to help real estate investors find the solutions and funds that best fits their needs.

Do not allow the fear of the unknown to stop you from becoming a real estate investor. Identify your interest, develop a strategy, and do not let anyone stand in the way of your dreams. You are in the driver's seat. Do not allow someone's negative experiences shape your future. As a real estate investor, you are taking the first step by seeking information. The more information you possess, the more confidence you will have in your abilities to strive for success in investing. Undoubtedly, there is an ebb and flow that accompanies any new endeavor, and investing in real estate is no different. You must be resilient, patient, and have a short memory if a deal falls through. It is easy to get frustrated as a real estate investor if you are not disciplined and practical. If real estate investors pursue a deal, it is because they see value and a way to make money from the deal.

It is human nature to search for ways to spend the potential windfall before the property closes and the check is cut. This is where discipline comes into play. Unlike most careers, there may be instances in which real estate investors will not be compensated, no matter how hard they work. I worked on a deal for nine months only to see it fall through. Instead of getting upset, you must move forward. There are too many deals and investment properties to walk away from investing all together, just because one deal fell though. If you break a plate, you do not stop using plates, correct? You just buy another one. This same principle applies to investing.

Competent real estate investors never put all their time, energy, and effort in one deal. Diversification is key. To be successful, master more than one area or type of real estate. Understand the changing needs and demographics of your market. Study the influences that cause shifts and stay ahead of the curve. Frustration comes from individuals who enter at the back end of a boom. The factors that caused the boom are dissipating, and competition is greater. You must learn how to become a visionary instead of following the herd. Ride the waves that come with real estate investing, but become savvy enough for them not to overtake you. Commitment is needed. You will be successful.

Do not lose focus of your goals and work diligently toward them. Steady gains will always be more satisfying than the thrill and devastation of exuberant gains followed by unexpected loss.

Chapter 2
BEGINNING STEPS: STARTING FROM SCRATCH

Congratulations on making the decision to become a real estate investor! Real estate investing is a worthwhile endeavor that can yield great benefits. This book is intended for people who are at the beginning or intermediate stage of their understanding of real estate investing. It is my goal that you will be able to use this book as a guide to get started or take your business to the next level. Most people are afraid to invest because they're dealing with fear, but there is nothing to be afraid of if you are properly prepared.

The first step in real estate investing is understanding where you are financially, which can be accomplished by meeting with a loan officer. While it is important to get a grasp of your financial situation in general, this first line of understanding may not with the person who ultimately finances your first project. Loan officers are a conduit of information to inform clients of their current financial situation and what steps need to be taken to achieve their goals. If you desire to pursue commercial investing, then a loan officer will be able to advise you on those loans. Conversely, if one decides to go into residential investing, a loan officer will be able to provide a tangible plan, as well. Financing is very important because many people are not able to pay cash out of pocket for the first investment. Many people do not have the upfront capital to go directly into investing.

When making a decision about the type of project to pursue, it is very important to shop around for the best possible interest rates and terms for the project. The lower the interest rate, the more money saved over a specified period. Furthermore, in order to get a good rate, the terms of the loans must be understood. For example, what is the required down payment for the loan? What are escalating fees for a loan? If the loan is paid off early, will there be a prepayment penalty? Another factor to consider is the ability to buy down points against the interest rate. Let's suppose one decides to purchase a home with at a 5 percent interest rate. A real estate investor can buy down the interest rate to 4 percent. For example, let's say $5,000 is set aside for every percentage point you buy down. If the rate is 5 percent, and one pays $5,000, the interest rate would be 4 percent. Although $5,000 is a nice chunk of money to pay upfront, it will pay for itself as part of a 30-year mortgage. In this case, $5,000 upfront can save a real estate investor thousands of dollars in the long run.

Another factor to consider asking potential lenders concerns special programs for real estate investors. There are programs for transactional lending, new construction, rehabilitation loans, first-time homebuyers, first-time flippers, and platforms for people with less than ideal credit, among others. No matter where your credit falls, ask about programs that can help begin your career as a real estate investor. Shop around to find the best financing package for your financial situation. It is imperative to ask the lender the ideal questions based upon your situation, such as your credit and real estate goals, to determine the best course of action. You can also inquire as to special programs lending institution may offer, some of which may not be typical for other clients. Take the time to research potential lenders that are not in your local area. You will be amazed to discover the different types of programs available for real estate investors.

If your credit is in good shape, you should approach a bank to extend a line of credit. Lines of credit allows real estate investors to gain access to a specified amount of money, which can be used to make purchases and repairs without taking out a specific loan on the property. If a real estate investor has a $500,000 open line of credit, he or she can purchase a home for $200,000, use $75,000 to renovate the home, then sell it for a profit at $400,000, if the value is there. Once the home has been sold, a real estate investor can pay back the $275,000 used from the open line of credit and keep the remaining $225,000 as profit. Using lines of credit is one of the best and easiest ways to purchase investment properties without running back and forth for approval letters from the lender. Open lines of credit are available for commercial and land acquisition purchases, as well.

The next important step is to find a competent and dependable realtor. I advise hiring a realtor that is investor-friendly. Every realtor does not have a desire to work with investors. because it involves patience, submitting multiple offers on the same property, and presenting offers that are far below the average market price. In essence, this means a realtor, per transaction, will be paid much less than average. An investor-friendly realtor will be open to doing multiple comparative market analyses, setting aside time in his or her schedule to show you multiple properties, and willing to submit multiple offers in a timely fashion. Patience is very important, and working with real estate investors takes time as well as trial and error. Do not be afraid to call real estate firms to ask who their most dependable, investor-friendly realtors are. Ask for references from their previous clients, as well.

The next step is to find a great home inspector or a licensed contractor who can give insight on the condition of the property. A good home inspector will be honest and take his or her time to analyze the property. Typically, real estate investors need two different inspectors: one for commercial real estate, and one for residential real estate investments. The cost of the inspection usually varies between residential and commercial inspections. I suggest interviewing potential home inspectors; these individuals will become an integral part of your team, and will help you determine which properties to purchase and which repairs will get the most value out of your investments.

One of the key factors in becoming a successful real estate investor is building strong relationships. In this field, relationships are worth more important than money. I have taken time to build relationships with my clients beyond receiving a check at closing. Real estate investors, in some markets, are a small group of people who often work with one another on transactions multiple times a year. For example, some agents may list only foreclosures, and others only work with commercial properties. Keeping open lines of communication with these agents can keep the negotiation process cordial, fun, and smooth for all parties involved. I have also found that having relationships with agents can help my investors to purchase property before it even hits the market. There are agents that I call to ask a simple question, such as "Do you have anyone who is thinking about listing a property that is on the fence about selling?" I follow up with telling them, "I have a buyer in a purchasing mode and looking to grab as much property as possible." This also works in instances in which a real estate investor sees a property and asks me to make a cold call to the property owner with an offer. Some of the best deals I have negotiated have been when a property is not on the open market. For a real estate investor, it reduces competition and surprises the potential seller by weighing the possibility of making money over holding on to a property.

By cultivating relationships with realtors and property owners, a real estate investor may begin to get calls about properties. Investors want to build a reputation for being the go-to person for purchasing property. You would be surprised at the calls I get from realtors and property owners to see if I have a client interested in a property. Even if a property is on the market, the calls let me know if there is little or no interest and the owner is desperate to sell. This is a great opportunity for my client to capitalize and negotiate a lower price.

Real estate investors must be able to build relationships with the local city government, as well. I highly advise real estate investors to attend city council meetings and get familiar with the zoning ordinances and future developments. Learning about new developments, businesses, and schools will become a road map to financial success. Knowing and understanding local changes will give you a boost to purchase property before the prices begin to inflate.

From time to time, stop by the city planner's office to see what changes are coming to your area. City planners are not able to give you street by street changes, but they will be able to suggest parts of town and/or inform you of new infrastructure that is being built. Always remember that cities and towns plan 5 to 20 years ahead; if you cannot see the value, trust the leadership to do what is in the best interest of the town and its growth.

One of the most fruitful meetings I have ever had was with a city planner. He told me that he could only circle areas on the map where development was taking place that might be of interest to investors. The city planner circled four areas, and I can honestly say his suggestions helped some of my clients make a lot of money.

I also want to suggest finding the local office that is responsible for economic development in your city. This is a great place to find grants and programs that offer incentives for real estate investors. The city that I reside in offers special loan programs for investing in redevelopment zones, and perks for investors who rent to low-income individuals. The economic development wing of local governments looks to build partnerships with local investors to help improve the quality of life in the city. This should not be overlooked.

The most important thing to remember when beginning this process is not stopping at "no." It is so easy to get disappointed, fall off track, and lose your focus. I'm telling you right now you will hear "no," and all your offers will not get accepted. Ignore negativity and always focus on the end game.

I highly recommend finding a mentor to guide you through the process of investing. Mentors can help you avoid mistakes and miscalculations they have made throughout their time as an investor. They can help you find lenders, contractors, and even the best areas to invest in property. Mentors are essential for your emotional and financial viability. I recommend not getting into real estate investing without a seasoned and competent mentor.

Remember, anything new takes practice and patience. When we were in kindergarten and first learned how to write, none of us could write a full paragraph. Growth and success come from time, patience, and learning from day-to-day challenges. There are two things that I can guarantee in this business: 1) if you properly strategize and execute your plan, you will be successful, and 2) disappointments may come, but you will be equipped, through this book, to overcome them. This book will help you develop a winning plan and strategies to persevere and buy another property.

Acquiring properties is a frequent, necessary occurrence in this industry. Do not get discouraged when you don't get a property, because there are other deals out there, and so many properties that will enter the market at any given time. In my current market, between 30 to 60 new properties enter the market every single day. Every day, there is a new potential for me to find a deal in either residential or commercial real estate. Don't get stuck if the deal does not work out. Stay encouraged and focused. Work with an investor-friendly realtor who can help keep the next deal in sight. Consistency, patience, and smart money moves will put you on the path to become the nation's next successful real estate investor.

Chapter 3
DEVELOPING YOUR INVESTING STRATEGY

While developing your strategy as a real estate investor, you must make sure your goals are attainable, measurable, and focused. Additionally, real estate investors must be prepared for what comes after the commitment. In any endeavor, there will be challenges, and investing in real estate is no different.

One of the best strategies that comes to mind is from a real estate investor I work with on the residential side. I actually began working with him by accident. I went to his office to sign some paperwork for another client who was purchasing a home from him. We struck up a conversation and after two meetings, I gained his business. His strategy is very particular, as he wants homes in horrible conditions. After we identify a property, he negotiates very hard to get the lowest possible price. After obtaining the home, he aims to sell it for three to fifteen thousand dollars more than what he paid for it. He does not repair the property and advertises that the home is in as-is condition. I have seen him do this on various occasions, and he is very proficient. The investors who purchase his homes view him as a man that can find deals. Even after he sells the properties, the investors are able to fix them and turn a healthy profit. Using this method, my client has a clear focus and a niche. I tried to introduce him to commercial real estate, but he simply said, "No thank you. I'm going to stick to these houses."

When successful real estate investors identify strategies that work, they should stick to them and avoid any distractions that may come. As I help investors on the commercial side, I recommended a building in an "ugly" condition, but he held true to what works for him. Similarly, the real estate investors that I work with on the commercial side of real estate investing are just as determined for success. I have an investor who couldn't care less about the condition of a building. This investor wants to know the net income, the cap rate, and a copy of the rent rolls for a potential purchase. He has purchased properties without physically going on a showing. He says, "If a building is making money, I can always fix it later. I need to know if a building is making money more than I know it needs repairs." By no means am I saying that investors cannot expand the reach of their strategy, but it is important to research multiple areas and create multiple scenarios.

When real estate investors prepare to develop their strategies, they need to consider the following factors:
1. Where do I want to invest?
2. What type(s) of property will be my focus?
3. What is my price point?
4. What is my market?
5. What is my exit strategy?

I have encountered investors who are not focused and operate outside of their strategy. As a realtor, I always make suggestions, but I cannot make investors stay on course; ultimately, I work for them. When an investor has an outlined strategy, focusing on successful deals is easier. For example, if a residential investor is looking for four-bedroom, two-bathroom homes under $150,000, in the red school district, in fair or poor condition, it makes it easier to say "no" to a home on another side of town in the blue school district that looks tempting, but will not yield the same equity as the residence in the red school district. By no means am I saying that investors cannot expand the reach of their strategy, but it is important for to research multiple areas and create multiple scenarios. Real estate investors must budget and have goals for their finances, before purchasing more property or investing in areas outside of real estate.

In addition, a strategy of a successful real estate investor should include the reinvestment into the next project. I would advise that 60 percent of the profits go back into the business. I make this suggestion because I have seen investors make $70,000 on a flip and forget that their profits are part of a strategy that is supposed to make them a millionaire. I encourage investors, when possible, to become less dependent on financing due to interest rates. Over time, interest rates work against a real estate investor's bottom line. I would like to see investors in a position to make cash purchases. I understand this is not possible for everyone. When real estate investors are able to make cash purchases, they can negotiate better deals with sellers, as sellers want to unload their properties as soon as possible. If sellers can get from under a property quicker because buyers have cash, they usually seize the opportunity.

Along with a strategy for investment, successful investors must include a strategy for their money, as well. Discipline is required to identify the correct property and reach financial success. One of the saddest faces I have seen on investors occurs after they have spent the profits from a flip, and don't know where and how they spent it. The importance of investing and saving beyond the closing is essential to success as an investor. Real estate investors must budget and have goals for their finances, be they purchasing more property or investing in areas outside of real estate.

Once the money begins to pour in, you must remember the reason you became a real estate investor. For some, the goal is to earn money to take care of their families, and set them up for financial freedom. The desire to help others in the community may be there, as well. Philanthropy is important, but do not forget to save yourself first; secure your own life vest before handing out life vests to others.

For those who desire to build a portfolio, or use real estate to wean themselves off full-time employment, I would suggest pursuing properties that will become rentals. Rental income is an excellent way to secure oneself financially; however, it takes more time to become established. While building a rental portfolio, real estate investors should purchase a home for every bill they have. If one home is not enough, then purchases more homes to cover a bill; this is usually typical of a car payment or mortgage. Once you have a home for each bill, then focus on building your portfolio to focus on how much you want as a cushion after all your bills are paid. This strategy can also be deployed in occasions in which one needs to pay off student loans or large medical bills. In my opinion, this is one of the smartest strategies for individuals who want to jump into real estate without taking a huge financial risk.

Many people look for magic formulas to make money. Over the course of history, there have been people who made fortunes by taking advantage of the blind desire of others to get rich. Real estate investing is a very useful tool in achieving wealth. However, very few people get rich quick by investing in real estate. The most successful real estate investors gain their wealth over time by making small calculated steps to financial success. There is no one way to make money in real estate; fortunes can be made in residential, commercial, and land transactions. While building a portfolio, I suggest trying multiple areas to find your niche. Understanding different areas of real estate investing and how they intersect will give an investor a greater understanding of how to multiply the potential earnings from a property.

To provide context, I have provided examples of individuals who have made a fortune from small and practical investments as real estate investors:

The Astor family became known for their wealth and dealings in real estate. Roughly 250 years ago, the Astor family began to transition from the fur trading business into purchasing land in what is now considered Manhattan in New York City. At the time, New York City, was surrounded by a bunch of farms and hamlets that did not seem very valuable. John Jacob Astor, the patriarch of the family, saw value in the waterways and trade routes that ran through the farms to city. To some, purchasing all those farms and hamlet seemed to prove worthless, but John Jacob Astor saw the value in buying large parcels that he would eventually subdivide and resell for a much larger profit. Through these real estate transactions, the Astor family became the first multi-millionaires in the United States. This money was eventually diversified and invested into other areas of business for the family, including the hotel industry. One of the most notable hotels in New York City today is the Waldorf Astoria, which is a symbol of their wealth and prominence in the city.

    Herman Russell purchased his first property when he was still in high school. Russell understood the importance of real estate investing, and used the profits from the sale of his first investment to pay for his college education. Russell went on to take over his father's plastering company, which he grew and transformed into a building and construction company. Russell is most notable for leveraging joint partnerships to fund real estate investments, and is also known as the man who built Atlanta, Georgia. Among some of the most famous buildings in the city built by Russell are the Georgia Dome, Hartsfield Jackson airport, Phillips Arena, and Turner Field. At the time of his retirement, Russell had built a conglomerate that featured construction, property management, and real estate development across the states of Alabama, Florida, Georgia, Louisiana, North Carolina, and Tennessee. This all came from a young man who had to struggle through segregation politics of the 1960s to become one of the wealthiest and most influential builders that this country has ever seen.

    Nowadays, the Buss family is known throughout the world for owning the Los Angeles Lakers. However, many people do not know that the patriarch of the family, Dr. Jerry Buss, built his fortune through real estate. Dr. Jerry Buss was born during the Great Depression and grew up in poverty. He saw real estate investing as a way to make more money for his family. Dr. Buss purchased his first property, a 14-unit multifamily dwelling, in 1954. He went on to purchase other properties and was instrumental in developing the city of Los Angeles. His plan of slow steady growth overtime led him to the ultimate business transaction of selling all his real estate holdings to purchase the Los Angeles Lakers, the L.A. Kings, and the Los Angeles Forum for $68 million. Today, the Los Angeles Lakers franchise is worth $2.7 billion. Furthermore, the most encouraging part of his story is that he only worked on real estate investing in the evenings and on the weekends while working in the education and aerospace engineering industries. Everyone who believes that part-time real estate investing does not pay off merely does not know the best way to pursue this field part time.

So, what will your story be? There are thousands, perhaps millions, of stories of men and women who have endeavored to make money from real estate. By setting a plan, they could focus and achieve the goals of financial freedom for their families. The stories I shared were few, but necessary in order to understand the great wealth that can be made from making simple decisions.

Anyone who seeks to become a real estate investor is making one of the best decisions of his or her life. It is possible to have everything you need and want, but you must be focused, determined, and dogmatic about seeing your dreams come to full fruition. Do not let any excuse, fear, or trepidation stop you. I look forward to reading about you one day, and learning about your story of overcoming adversity and fear. Don't become someone who simply talks about the great ideas, but never puts them into practice.

One of my favorite things to do is speak with older people about all the things that they wish they had done throughout their lives. I always make note of what they say, as I see these stories as a gateway both into failure and into my own success. By learning about the failures, trials, and success of others, you can make great strides in becoming one of the next great, success stories. Starting with modest beginnings in real estate, you, too, can make a substantial impact on the world.

Chapter 4
RESIDENTIAL INVESTING BASICS

Residential real estate for the purpose of this guide will include single-family homes and one- to four-unit multi-family homes. Multi-family homes five units and over classify as commercial real estate in the state of North Carolina. Check your state guidelines to verify the regulations for your state. Generally speaking, financing for single-family homes and one- to four-unit multi-family homes works the same. We will discuss this in more detail later in the chapter.

When investing in residential real estate, one must always consider the market:

1. What are the needs of the market?
2. Are any businesses coming to or leaving my town?
3. What is the range of sales and rental price points?
4. What style home best fits the market demographics?
5. What areas are blighted and scheduled for a comeback, according to city planners?

The needs of every market can vary. As a real estate investor, finding the needs of your local community can give you an edge with a niche market. If you are in a town with an influx of college students, you should do well with purchasing and renting properties. If you are in a market with an aging population, you may want to invest in homes and apartments that can accommodate the needs of this population. In the 55 and up demographic, many are looking for ranch style homes with wide doorways and spacious hallways. Many in this demographic are looking to downsize to a smaller home or duplex. If you are in a market in which jobs and industries are leaving, you may want to focus on renting instead of flipping homes. If employers are leaving your market without other industries stepping in to provide employment, you will most likely find homes in foreclosure, or sellers in a distressed situation. One will be able to purchase these homes at a below market value and rent them to those who cannot afford a down payment on a home, or have bad credit due to losing a job. I am not making light of individuals in dire situations, but I see these situations occur all the time. Savvy investors can be compassionate while positioning themselves to get ahead of the market.

In my market, there are a lot of military families. The rental and new construction segments of the market are booming. There are development companies that are doing very well within this market. Another sub-market that ties into the rental market consist of investors who flip homes. There is a growing number of military retirees that settle in my market; they have disposable income and want to spend it wisely. In some instances, investing in real estate is great for them. Some focus on buying and renting homes to supplement their income while they are still serving our country.

So, how do investors know they are getting the best deal, or making an offer that will position them for financial success? You can be confident if you keep the following in mind when presenting an offer for a residential property:

1. Buy the worst home in the best neighborhood.

The cheapest residential properties are frequently located in communities or areas that are not desirable, and do not meet the average needs of the market. Generally speaking, it will be difficult to command a rent that near the market average, and flipping will be difficult because much of the area is blighted, rendering the comps useless. Let's suppose one finds a three-bedroom, two-bath home for $9,900 in a neighborhood with homes with a median value of $35,000. In addition, let's say that this property needs repairs that total $20,000. Already, the home is costing the investor nearly $30,000 without considering listing fees, carrying costs, advertising, and the possibility of paying closing costs. In this case, the best option would be to rent the property. Unless the area was slated to be improved in some way by the city, this would be a perfect example of flipping in the wrong area.

On the other hand, finding a home for $60,000 in a community with residences with a median value of $225,000 that requires $20,000 worth of repairs would place the investor in a great situation to maximize the equity in the home when compared to the previous scenario. The latter residence will benefit from the value of every home around it.

When it comes to finding in equity in rent, the overall goal is to make a profit after mortgage payment and potential property management fees are taken out. If an investor has a home that costs $1,000 per month in mortgage payments, and the property management fee is 10 percent, rental fees to the tenant should be at least $1,200, if the market allows. If the average rent in the market is $1,800 per month, and the property management fee is $180 per month as a result, then the investor would earn $620 in profit per month after the mortgage payment. Investors always want to make certain they are making no less than a 30 percent profit on the rental per month. Furthermore, it is also wise to have three months of the mortgage payment saved per rental to make certain you can cover the cost of the home if finding a tenant proves to be difficult.

2. Position your investment in the market.

Two mistakes investors make are overvaluing and overpricing their residential properties. Popular upgrades must be done in relation to value, in an ideal situation. Investors must have a desire to make money, but not to a point in which greed blinds them and leads them to list their properties improperly. Every real estate investor needs to know the appraisal value of their homes as well as the market value through a comparative market analysis (CMA). A CMA can be executed for free by a licensed realtor. A good CMA will consider how an investor's home stacks up in the market, and will take into consideration the age, construction type, features, and size of a residence to give a median value and range. Once an investor knows the range, he or she can place the home on the market.

I ask my investors to consider one of two options when pricing their properties: position their home prices toward the middle of the market, or list their residences two to five percent less than the appraisal price if stuck on a numerical value for their investment. The number one objective is to have a successful flip that allows the investor to make money and move on to the next project; moving on is difficult the longer a home sits on the market. A good realtor will help identify homes that are affordable with features the buyer desires for a reasonable price. Following these tips will help ensure that your investment is attractive in price not only to the buyer, but to the realtor, as well. Investors must understand that various clients want certain features and amenities in a residence, but within a particular price point. Realtors then attempt to find homes to fit the criteria desired by their clients. If an investor's home is priced and positioned correctly, it will be easier for a realtor to present it to a buyer. The last thing you want is for a realtor to overlook a property because it is overpriced. Investors must give themselves a chance to receive showings on their investments. The first step in this process is making the home financially attractive.

3. Be conservative with repairs and updates.

I advise real estate investors, especially new investors, to do minimum repairs on their first one to three flips before tackling major rehab projects that will require tearing down walls, adding rooms, and/or require major plumbing and electrical work. Major repairs can be costly, especially if one is inexperienced. A costly rehab project may deter new investors from future projects. I encourage lip-stick flips, which just need cosmetic work before placing back on the market. Lip-stick flips are easier to afford, and generally consist of replacing carpet, updating flooring, painting walls, repairing holes in drywall, landscaping, updating fixtures, and replacing appliances. I often suggest these improvements, especially in a home that has the desired rooms and square footage.

In some cases, real estate investors can become overwhelmed with what they see on television, and what they feel they must duplicate when flipping properties. I always advise investors to enlist the services of a licensed home inspector during the due diligence process to determine what needs to be fixed in a home prior to taking possession. When one feels confident enough to tackle more difficult projects, make certain that the proper permits are gathered by a licensed general contractor. Generally speaking, each phase of repairs, electrical work, plumbing, and foundation needs to be inspected before moving on with other repairs. However, investors are at the mercy of the inspector's schedule, which can cause delays in completions. Make sure that carrying costs are included, and that your schedule can absorb possible delays in the repair schedule.

Financing for single-family homes can be achieved in a myriad of ways. If an investor does not have 20 percent to put down on a conventional loan for a property, I would suggest considering a FHA loan. Credit unions have various programs that can be customized to home buyers, as well. Banks are also a good source of funding, especially if you have a prior relationship with a particular financial institution, which consists of established accounts in good standing. Private equity lending is available, as well. However, investors must do their due diligence when it comes to private equity lending. Private equity, depending on the lender, can be very creative with terms such as down payment, length, interest rates, and buying down points. Terms are negotiable, but the interest rates tend to be higher. I would suggest private equity for short term lending only, and not as a substitute for lending on a single-family or one- to four-unit residence for more than two years. Ideally, cash is the easiest and cheapest way to purchase a property, as it bypasses the interest rates, finance charges, and mortgage insurance that accompany many loans. Furthermore, cash deals can be easier to negotiate, and may give a seller motivation to make a deal.

When financing one- to four-unit residences, current rent payments may help an investor get approved for lending. If a tenant is in place, an investor can count the rent toward the probability of income when qualifying for a purchase. In the case of one- to four-family units, most banks and financial institutions will not consider the possibility of income if there are no tenants residing in the property. This question is often asked to potential investors, and it's important to understand the reality of the situation. Most banks and financial institutions feel that there is no guarantee an investor will find a tenant, and do not want to give financial consideration for a family that is not occupying a property at the time of purchase, although the investor has every intention on filling the vacancy. One- to four-family units are excellent because they are considered to be one building, and are treated equally to single-family residences.

For an investor that is able, it would be advantageous to live in one of the units while renting the others to build their finances to pursue another property. As an example, consider having a mortgage of $850 a month, but collecting $900 per month from three other tenants for a net monthly income of $1850 after the mortgage is paid. Depending on an investor's market, the net monthly income can be exponentially more.

Chapter 5
LAND INVESTING BASICS

For real estate investors, land investments can be tricky. Land is one of the hardest commodities to value, but it can produce a tremendous rate of return. Land is difficult to value because its soil evaluation, flood determination, topography, and distance from utilities need to be considered along with its acreage and zoned usage.

As a rule of thumb, land holds more value once it is developed and/or improved. Land is considered improved once a building or infrastructure, such as roads, sewer, or utility lines, have been laid. Land possesses many different types of investment potentials. Other improvements aside from buildings can be the addition of billboards, cell phone towers, solar panels, or wind turbines.

Regarding all potential investments, make certain that the local jurisdiction will allow for its particular usage. Billboards and cellphone towers can create great opportunities for residual incomes, from renting to regional and national companies. The average investment for billboards is between

$75,000 and $150,000, but an owner may command a lease payment of $2,500 to $7000 per month, depending on the location. Wind turbines and solar panels are both used to harness energy and are increasing in popularity. Government-sponsored grants are available to help purchase the equipment needed to profile electricity to a business or subdivision.

Nevertheless, undeveloped land holds earning potential, as well. If investors own or purchase a large enough tract of land, they can charge a fee for seasonal passes on their property for activities like camping, hunting, or fishing. In wooded areas, paintball courses are gaining popularity throughout the country. As a real estate investor, there is also money in selling timber and logging rights, as logging companies will pay land owners to cut timber from their property. This is very useful if one purchases a tract of land that is heavily wooded that they want to use for a subdivision without paying for the cost of clearing the land themselves.

Subdividing land is one of the most popular forms of making money on a vacant tract of land. Let's say that a real estate investor purchases a 10-acre tract of land for $50,000.

Suppose the typical home lot size is 0.20 acres, for the purpose of this scenario. Residence lots in your market sell for $15,000 apiece. Due to required obstructions, streets, and sidewalks, you will lose roughly two acres of the land to improvements. This will leave an investor with eight acres to sell. At $15,000 per lot, an investor is looking to make $75,000 per acre. If a real estate investor sells all eight acres, the gross income is $600,000 prior to subtracting the original investment, permits, and construction costs.

Having land in an investment portfolio is very important. Land can cost very little, but can jump exponentially in value when in demand. If one does not want to sell their land, it can be leased. Many Fortune 500 restaurant chains sign ground leases for $5,000 to $9,000 per month. A new model for positioning restaurants is being leveraged near Wal-Mart and Target shopping centers, in which chain restaurants are placed in front of major stores to capitalize on the flow of traffic, and will sign long-term leases to secure a location.

Ground leases can be beneficial for various uses. I once advised a family on the verge of selling a 12-acre tract of land for $150,000 to their county for burial plots. After the usage was known, the family decided to lease the land, and negotiated a rate of $22,000 per month.

Acquiring land is a transaction of patience. Even when an investor cannot directly benefit from the investment during his or her life, it may be a tremendous blessing to future generations.

Chapter 6
COMMERCIAL INVESTING BASICS

Commercial properties are high risk and high reward. Investors like commercial properties because their earning potential is greater than residential properties for a similar investment. In my market, a 1500-square foot home purchased for $100,000 can rent for $750 to $900 a month. However, a commercial space purchased for the same price and of equal square footage would rent for $1500 to $2200 or more per month. With the added potential value, commercial properties tend to cost more to repair than residential properties. Commercial properties tend to sit on the market longer than residential properties. However, businesses tend to stay in one location and sign longer leases, as well.

Value for commercial property is usually determined by its usage, zoning, parking, and attached acreage that may be used for future development. If one desires to invest in commercial properties, keep the building a shell with very little customization. This will make it easier for the tenant to make the necessary changes to conform to their business usage. Commercial investments can take on many forms, from apartment complexes to medical offices and even churches. The possibilities for tenants are limitless. A new real estate investor may want to consider the following as targets for investing to get their feet wet: storage units, shopping centers, business centers, daycares, counseling facilities, retail spaces, and rooms for conference/meeting spaces.

When identifying a building for a commercial location, consider the following:
1. Traffic Count- The number of vehicles passing a location on a daily basis. This can be found at the website of the state department of transportation. This is very important because it can help determine the likelihood of potential customers to a renter.
2. Income of the Community- Does the average income of the community allow for disposable income that may contribute to supporting businesses that I may attract to lease my building?
3. Average Education- Companies may use this as a factor for their potential workforce prior to leasing a location.

4. Surrounding Businesses: What is the competition for leasing space in the area? Is there a missing niche business that one's building can draw?
5. Additional Acreage: Is there land that I can develop to take advantage of the traffic of an existing business? E.g., Wal-Mart, K-Mart, shopping mall.
6. Growing Residential Development: Is there a new or growing subdivision that will need restaurants, convenience stores, and shops?
7. Lack of Residential Development: Can I build a subdivision or apartment complex for people who want to live closer to their favorite restaurants and shops?

For real estate investors who want to diversify their portfolio with one purchase, you may be able to purchase a business/building combination. In some instances, property owners don't only want to part ways with a building, but with the connected business, as well. I have seen this occur with daycares, medical offices, home health agencies, real estate companies, and barbershops. If one runs into this potential, always negotiate to keep the existing clients and/or contracts; this will be one less hurdle for an investor to navigate on the way to financial success.

Financing for commercial properties varies and can get creative. Typically, down payments on commercial deals can range from 15 to 30 percent. The lowest down payment I've encountered while helping a client purchase a building was 5.5 percent.

The types of loans can vary as well, as balloon, assumptions, and seller financing are all on the table. There are also opportunities for private equity lending, but similar to residential lending, the interest rates are higher. If one is purchasing a building that has tenants, make sure to ask for the rent rolls and the terms of the leases. As the potential owner, you need to determine how much longer the tenants will be in place, what they are paying in rent and other fees, and their options at the end of the current lease. A real estate investor also needs to know if the current property management company will continue to provide services. I suggest that every investor uses the services of a property management company to vet potential renters, collect rent payment, arrange repairs, and evict tenants, if necessary, as investors should not have to deal with hassles that may result from dealing directly with the tenants. Property management companies are also responsible for advertising the property itself, which is done for a fee that is determined by the company and the owner of the property.

One common mistake in commercial investing is purchasing a residential building, a house that is zoned for commercial usage. This is a point of contention that often leads to disputes over the value of the building. Some property owners believe if their home is zoned for commercial use, then it is a commercial building. My contention has always been that a house is a house. The cost of materials to build a commercial building is different in many regards. I advise real estate investors to proceed with caution unless the building was renovated to fit commercial needs for ADA accessibility, medical uses, or for any specialized usage. If a building has not been completely renovated for professional usage, then the building is a house, and the comps used to determine its value needs to reflect this fact.

Another factor to consider regarding the overall cost

of a commercial investment is the potential costs that may arise due to environmental factors. If one desires to pursue a property such as a carwash, gas station, or an auto-body repair shop, make sure one is aware of the costs that may be associated with environmental hazards such as contamination of the soil or ground water.

The Environmental Protection Agency (EPA) is very serious in making sure the environment is protected from potential hazards that can be produced by industrial and commercial usage. Before making a purchase, always get an inspection and be aware of the risks as well as remedies. Real estate investors should carry an insurance policy that is commiserate with the type of industry provided by the property. In some cases, a one-million-dollar policy will be sufficient, whereas others should carry at least a five-million-dollar policy. The amount required to carry may be determined by the insurance company. Carrying a multi-million dollar policy may sound expensive, but in actuality, it may only cost the real estate investor a few hundred dollars a month, which is a small expense in the scope of the entire investment.

Appendix A
ECONOMIC DEVELOPMENT THROUGH REAL ESTATE

Economic development can be achieved through real estate. There are many issues that exist within communities throughout the country. Successful real estate investors will have the time and resources to positively impact their communities.

Below is an outline to help develop programs to focus on the needs of one's community, and the benefits that may result from implementing initiatives.

However, I would advise against starting any program without providing classes or seminars to increase the understanding of the needs of the target population.

Community Needs:

Every community has deficiencies that need to be addressed beyond a policy level. Savvy real estate investors can use their knowledge of investing to help provide services to provide a two-fold solution to provide assistance and financially benefit the community. Below are a few examples of housing programs that can create excellent opportunities to partner with local municipalities.

- Transitional Homes for Veterans, Widows, the Unemployed, and the Homeless
- Solutions for Child Poverty
- Solutions for Senior Citizens in Poverty
- Solutions for the Disabled

Benefits (Mindset)

Many investors see the desire to go a step further to help those who are hesitant to invest in real estate, as they are often presented with the following question: "How were you able to take advantage of real estate to make so much money?" Below are a few benefits of mentoring potential real estate investors, and the necessary characteristics to develop a mindset for real estate investing.
- Financial Literacy
- Confidence

- Improved Perception of the Community
- Work vs. Building Wealth

Education (Seminars)

What I have discussed are suggestions for you to succeed. Although these methods are tried and true, you may discover a few additional tips that help you reach the next level. If so, share this information, as your advice may help others to accomplish their investing goals. Everyone is different; some people succeed with 21 steps to success, while others can only absorb 3 to reach their best output.

Below you will find areas that can help to bring awareness, clients, and additional income to real estate investors.

- Goal Setting
- Budgeting
- Credit Improvement
- Home Buying and Investing

Job Creation

As an investor, you are encouraging and contributing to the interest in real estate. If you decide to merge your interest in this exciting field with a more secure income, you may want to consider the following areas to complement your ongoing real estate business.

- Agent-Residential Brokerage
- Agent-Commercial Brokerage
- Agent-Industrial Brokerage
- Agent-Farm and Land Brokerage
- Real Estate Appraising
- Property Management
- Land Development
- Urban Planning
- Real Estate Counseling
- Real Estate Research

APPENDIX B
TIPS FOR NEGOTIATING

Negotiating in real estate is very important. However, beating competing offers is even more important. Sellers are savvy about their properties, the market, and typical buyer tactics. Knowing the answer to the following questions can help you negotiate a real estate transaction.

Know the Facts

1. How long has the property been on the market?

If a home has not been on the market long, the property owner is less likely to negotiate the price of the home. However, what is considered to be a long time on the market for a particular property? In some markets, property sellers expect their listing to be off of the market in 90 days, and in other cases, a year. Find out the parameters and be prepared to make an offer based upon the willingness for a seller to get the property off his or her hands.

2. **Are there any perceived undesirable defects with the property?**

For example, if a home is in a flood zone, this may help an investor in negotiating. Furthermore, a home inspection also will uncover any potential defects with the home. Always attain the services of a licensed home inspector, and do not be afraid to ask for repairs or a lower asking price. In the event of a foreclosure that is sold in as-is condition, make certain to factor in the potential of unseen damage in your price. Do not be hesitant to present an offer that is well below market value.

3. **How desirable is the community and/or school system?**

Real estate is all about location. Curb appeal is not the only exterior factor that can help or hinder a property. Investors should be reluctant to present an offer on a property that is not in a stellar community and/or school system. A property in a sub-par location can affect resale value and the potential to rent.

4. Is the property under distress (foreclosure/short sale)?

If a property is distressed via foreclosure, you can begin negotiating the price between 9 to 13 percent of the asking price in many locales. In some areas, you can go even lower. A branch manager at a credit union in North Carolina once told me that he had lost as much as 40 percent on foreclosed properties. Investors should never feel bad about taking advantage of these truths. Properties under distress are opportunities to help investors build their portfolios.

5. Are properties in the area selling over/under list price?

The ideal situation is to pay as little as possible for the greatest potential gain, but there are exceptions. In some instances, properties in desirable areas sell above asking price. If a real estate investor is at the bottom of an upward swing, there is still time for him or her to capitalize on financial gains, even when paying above the asking price for an investment. Knowing this will help real estate investors turn a profit when purchasing premium properties.

6. Will the owner of the home consider seller financing?

An investor may have to offer full asking price if a property is priced correctly in the market. If this occurs, negotiate other terms and conditions, such as closing costs, possession, repairs, upgrades, and warranties. Pay attention to the trends in your community; every market is different.

7. How can assignments benefit me, as a real estate investor?

If you find a property that has value, but you are not in position to purchase it, an assignment can be a valuable tool. By yielding permission to an investor from the seller to market and sell the property, an assignment can allow an investor to purchase the property from the seller at one price, then sell it at a much higher price on the open market. For example, an investor can enter an agreement on assignment for $150,000, but ultimately market and sell the property for $275,000.

Transactional funds can be used to purchase the residence on the front-end agreement and pay it off with a back-end transaction. Even if the property never sells, investors are not obligated to purchase the property, and it reverts back to the original owner.

Assignments, from my experience, work well on vacant and abandoned properties. Banks are not willing to perform assignments on foreclosed properties.

Appendix C
MINING FOR DIAMONDS: FINDING THE NEXT DEAL

Investing in real estate requires patience. Through patience, savvy, and a willingness to step outside of the box, you can find ways to get ahead of the competition and find untapped resources in the market. Below, you will find tips to locate great prices in your area.

1. **Find what's next.**

This sounds easy, but it can be very difficult if you are not paying attention to the market. Investing in land is very important. Whenever an investor notices growth in business and/or certain industries, a location to build institutions such as schools and retail, medical, and governmental offices and subdivisions is not too far behind. Purchasing property in rural areas or locations that are on the outskirts of urban areas is essential for an investor to take advantage of an untapped earning potential. As an example, it is well known that the Astor family of New York diversified its wealth by purchasing farms and homesteads in what is now known as Manhattan.

As William Backhouse Astor said, "Purchase in acres, sell in lots."

2. **Find a distressed property that is poised for a comeback.**

Pride can drive an investor to make a horrible decision if he or she is not focused on factors to create a strong return on investment. Distressed areas can be urban or rural that were vital for business, industry, and state identity and/or image. In other words, there will be an interest in an area, but will this interest prompt city leaders and business owners with a desire to see the city go beyond its previous glory? Whenever mayors and city councils start voting to offer incentives for businesses to relocate, get ready to begin spending. This is an excellent opportunity for an investor to start purchasing property that will be worth exponentially more within the next three to ten years. Detroit, Michigan, is a perfect example of this phenomenon, as is Brooklyn, New York, around the Barclays Center. If an investor is not in position to purchase and hold the property, I would advise him or her to stay away from this type of investment, especially if it is his or her first investment. Occasionally, real estate investors believe they can turn an area around alone; in some cases, they are the only individuals who want to see an area improve. However, it is very important to be able to separate feelings and emotions from investments. The best investments make money; not fulfill emotional or nostalgic needs.

3. Ask uncomfortable questions.

Questions need to be asked internally, which, in turn, will provoke an investor to move externally.

An investor once asked me where he could find solid rentals in our community. He was very specific in wanting homes that were well built and in settled neighborhoods. Internally, I asked myself, "What neighborhoods were once the most desired, but have an aging population?" In various neighborhoods, several military retirees had settled down throughout the area. Although I am very fond of the community that I work in, many of the children of the military retires do not want to live in the homes their parents lived in. I noticed a steady stream of homes going into foreclosure that were paid off, but had unpaid taxes. In these cases, parents had passed away and their children were not willing to pay taxes on a home in an area in which they did not wish to return. I took this as an opportunity not only to give my client valuable insight, but also to figure out what I could do before these homes went into foreclosure.

Plans for a residence often go ignored when a loved one is sick or terminally ill, but this presents an opportunity for an investor. I am not trying to be morbid, but this is a reality that needs to be discussed. Furthermore, although asking about the plans for a property may sound insensitive, making an offer to a family who may need money for medical expenses can be a blessing.

Nevertheless, I would suggest allowing the infirmed to live in the home until their death, and only take possession of the residence afterward. The last thing an investor wants to be is an inconsiderate, heartless being who makes sick people leave their homes. In this situation, asking an uncomfortable question will give an investor time to eliminate competition from other investors, provide resources for a family, and negotiate the price before the individual's successors greedily profit from its sale, especially if the residence is paid off.

4.   Research, study, and apply.

There is no point of having useful information and not using it. Many people know it is beneficial to purchase foreclosed properties, but they believe it is too risky and takes too much work. When I first started working with investors in real estate, many deals were available via courthouse foreclosures. I believe these properties offer priceless opportunities they to investors of all kinds. However, investors and/or their agents must be willing to spend time researching properties to see if they will be a good fit.

All foreclosed properties are public knowledge and easy to access. An amortization calculator can be used to tell an investor how much principal cost is left on the loan. I advise investors to pursue properties that have received a bid. If there were no bids on the property, then the county holds the bid. This means either there is not much interest in a property, or that someone is observing and waiting to see what will happen. After a property has received a bid, there is usually an upset period to give investors time to place an offer. Another reason that I advise investors to only bid on properties that have been auctioned is because some owners of foreclosures meet the terms of the bank to stop the process, and the property never sees the courthouse steps. Therefore, this will help an investor not waste time with research or paying for title searches to make sure the property has no liens.

All county and city actions of real property are subject to liens. I suggest spending money on a title search if you are confident the investment will be worth it. Many county and city offices do not have time to perform lien searches, so they do not depend on them to provide advice. If investors are knowledgeable, or have an experienced agent, they may be able to determine if the foreclosed property has liens on file.

In the same vein of research, knowing the tax value is not enough to determine if a foreclosure is an excellent purchase. Real estate investors are unable to access the property, so they must assume the worst and hope for the best when it comes to its interior condition. Once again, this is when research comes into play. The average sales price for a subdivision as well as the average cost per square foot for a certain area can be discovered with knowledge, patience, and proper resources. Once a real estate investor is armed with this information, he or she can be very effective in bidding on foreclosed property.

5.   Develop a strong marketing strategy.

Once investors have found their diamond-in-the-rough properties, they must be creative to advertise it. The multiple listing service (MLS) is not the only way to advertise, but it is a good start. When listing a property through an agent, the property will eventually end up on hundreds of aggregate sites that have partnerships with the local MLS. Sites like home.com, realtor.com and Zillow.com pull their listings from such relationships. Over 80 percent of homebuyers begin their search for residences online. Social media is the new marketing tool that is beginning to benefit investors. Why? Individuals who may see pictures of your property can instantly share them with hundreds or thousands of friends with a click of a button. This type of exposure cannot be frowned upon. However, one must be knowledgeable about the sites to locates potential buyers.

Although Instagram is very popular, sites such as Facebook, Twitter, and Pinterest will be better suited towards potential property buyers because of the targeted age group of each site. Another great way to advertise a home is though eBay and Craigslist.

Although real estate investors' properties may be listed at market value, some individuals might believe they are getting a better deal because the listings are on sites that are known for great prices. In the end, perception is the best tool to sell a property. Perception of price, value, presentation, and condition help investors earn the best price for their investments.

Appendix D
COMMON REAL ESTATE TERMS AND DEFINITIONS

A

ABANDONMENT –

The voluntary surrender or relinquishment of possession of real property with the intention of terminating one's possession or interest, but without vesting this interest in any other person.

ABSTRACT OF TITLE –

A concise, summarized history of the title to a specific parcel of real property, together with a statement of all liens and encumbrances affecting the property. The abstract of title doesn't guarantee or assure the validity of the title of the property. It merely discloses those items about the property which are of public record, and thus doesn't reveal such things as encroachments, forgeries, and the like.

ACRE –

A measure of land equaling 43,560 square feet; 4,840 square

yards; 160 square rods.

AD VALOREM –

Latin for "according to valuation," usually referring to a type of tax or assessment.

ADJUSTABLE-RATE MORTGAGE (ARM) –

A mortgage loan where the interest rate, initially fixed, begins to fluctuate after a certain amount of time based on some financial index, usually on an annual basis.

ADVERSE POSSESSION –

The acquiring of title to real property owned by someone else, by means of open, notorious, and continuous possession for the statutory period of time (20 years in Hawaii).

AFFIDAVIT –

A sworn statement reduced to writing and made under oath before a Notary Public or other official authorized by law to administer an oath.

AGREEMENT OF SALE –

An agreement between the seller (vendor) and buyer (vendee) for the purchase of real property.

ALLOWANCES –
In construction or remodeling, a line item in the contractor's bid when the exact product, brand, or cost is yet to be determined. An estimate or placeholder for an expense.

AMENITIES –
Features, both tangible and intangible, which enhance and add to the desirability of real estate.

AMERICANS WITH DISABILITIES ACT (ADA) –
First enacted in 1990, ADA is a broad-based civil rights law that prohibits discrimination based on physical or mental disability. Among its many provisions, ADA requires that most public facilities meet certain accessibility guidelines. "ADA compliant" means that the product, fixture, or material meets the standards as outlines by the act.

AMORTIZATION –
The gradual repayment of a debt by means of systematic pay-

ments of principal and interest over a set period, where at the end of the period there is a zero balance.

ANNUAL PERCENTAGE RATE –
The relationship of the total finance charge to the total amount to be finance as required under the Federal Truth-in-Lending Law.

APPRAISAL –
The process of estimating, fixing, or setting the market value of real property. An appraisal may take the form of a lengthy report, a completed form, a simple letter, or even an oral report.

APPRECIATION –
An increase in the worth or value of property due to economic or related causes, which may prove to be either temporary or permanent.

ASSESSED VALUATION –
The value of real property as established by the state government for purposes of computing real property taxes.

ASSESSMENT –

A specific levy for a definite purpose, such as adding curbs or sewers in a neighborhood.

ASSIGNMENT –

The transfer of the right, title, and interest in the property of one person, the assignor, to another, the assignee. In real estate, there are assignments of mortgages, contracts, agreements of sale, leases, and options, among others.

ASSUMPTION OF MORTGAGE –

The act of acquiring title to property, which has an existing mortgage on it, and agreeing to be personally liable for the terms and conditions of the mortgage, including payments.

B

BALLOON PAYMENT –

The final payment of a note or obligation, which is substantially larger than the previous installment payments, and which repays the debt in full; the remaining balance, which is due at the maturity of a note or obligation.

BASIS –

The financial interest which IRS attributes to the owner of an asset for purposes of determining annual depreciation and gain or loss on sale of the asset.

BILL OF SALE –

A written agreement by which one person sells, assigns, or transfers his right to, or interest in, personal property to another.

BOUNDARIES –

The perimeters or limits of a parcel of land as fixed by legal description which is usually a metes and bounds description.

BREACH OF CONTRACT –

Violation of any of the terms or conditions of a contract without legal excuse; default, non-performance, such as failure to make payment when due.

BUILDING PERMIT –

A written permission granted by the County Building Department and required prior to beginning the construction of a new building or other improvement (including fences, fence walls, retaining walls and swimming pools).

C

CAPITAL GAIN –
The taxable profit derived from the sale of a capital asset.

CAPITAL IMPROVEMENT –
Any structure that's erected as a permanent improvement to real property; any improvement that's made to extend the useful life of a property, or to add to the value of the property.

CERTIFICATE OF REASONABLE VALUE (CRV) –
A certificate issued by the Veterans Administration setting forth a property's current market value estimate, based upon a VA approved appraisal.

CHAIN OF TITLE –
The recorded history of matters that affect the title to a specific parcel of real property, such as ownership, encumbrances, and liens, usually beginning with the original recorded source

of the title.

CHANGE ORDERS –

In remodeling or construction, when a change is made to construction materials or a plan.

CLEAR TITLE –

Title to property that's free from liens, defects, or other encumbrances, except those which the buyer has agreed to accept, such as mortgage to be assumed, the ground lease of record, and the like; established title; title without clouds.

CLOSING –

The final stage of consummating a real estate transaction when the seller delivers title to the buyer, in exchange for the purchase price.

CLOSING COSTS –

Expenses of the sale which must be paid in addition to the purchase price (in the case of the buyer's expenses), or be deducted from the proceeds of the sale (in the case of the seller's expenses).

CLOSING STATEMENT –

A detailed cash accounting of a real estate transaction prepared by an escrow officer or other person designated to process the mechanics of the sale, showing all cash that was received, all charges and credits which were made, and all cash that was paid out in the transaction; also called a settlement statement.

CLOUDED TITLE –

Any document, claim, unreleased lien or encumbrance which may impair or injure the title to property or make the title doubtful because of its apparent or possible validity.

CLUSTER DEVELOPMENT –

The grouping of housing units on less than normal size home sites, with the remaining land being devoted to common areas.

COLLATERAL –

Something of value given or pledged as security for a debt or obligation. The collateral for a real estate mortgage loan is the mortgaged property itself, which has been hypothecated.

COMMON AREAS –

Land or improvements designated for the use and benefit of all residents, property owners, and tenants.

COMPARABLES –

Recently sold properties, which are similar to a particular property being evaluated, and which are used to indicate a reasonable fair market value for the subject property.

COMPOUND INTEREST –

Interest which is computed upon the principal sum plus accrued interest.

CONDEMNATION –

Either a judicial or administrative proceeding to exercise the power of eminent domain, i.e., the power of the government to take private property for public use.

CONTINGENCY –

A provision placed in contract that requires the completion of a certain act or the happening of a particular event before a contract is binding.

CONTRACT –

A legal agreement between competent parties who agree to perform or refrain from performing certain acts for a consideration. In real estate, there are many different types of contracts, including listings, contracts of sale, options, mortgages, assignments, leases, deeds, escrow agreements, and loan commitments, among others.

CONVENTIONAL LOAN –

A type of mortgage loan made by a bank or other financial institution on its own terms, not underwritten by a government-insured program such as FHA or VA. Conventional loans can be both conforming--written to the underwriting standards set by Fannie Mae and Freddie Mac--or nonconforming.

CONVEYANCE –

The transfer of title to real property by means of a written instrument, such as a deed or an assignment of lease.

COUNTEROFFER –

A new offer made as a reply to an offer received from another;

this has the effect of rejecting the original offer, which cannot thereafter be accepted unless revived by the offeror's repeating it.

COVENANT –
A written agreement or promise of two or more parties by which either pledges to perform or not to perform specified acts on a property, or which specifies certain uses or non-uses of the property.

COVENANTS AND CONDITIONS –
Covenants are promises contained in contracts, the breach of which would entitle a person to damages. Conditions, on the other hand, are contingencies, qualifications, or occurrences upon which an estate or property right would be gained or lost.

D

DEALER –
An IRS designation for a person who regularly buys and sells real property.

DECLARATION OF RESTRICTIONS –

A statement of all the covenants, conditions, and restrictions ("CC&R's") that affect a parcel of land.

DEED –

A written instrument by which a property owner "grantor" transfers to a "grantee" an ownership in real property.

DEED OF TRUST –

A legal document in which title to property is transferred to a third-party trustee as security for an obligation owed by the trustor (borrower) to the beneficiary (lender).

DEFAULT –

Failure to fulfill a duty or promise or failure to perform any obligation or required act. The most common occurrence of default on the part of a buyer or lessee is non-payment of money.

DENSITY –

A term, frequently used in connection with zoning requirements, which means the maximum number of building units per acre or the number of occupants or families per unit of land area (acre, square mile, etc.); usually the ratio of land area to improvement area.

DEVELOPER –

One who attempts to put land to its most profitable use by the construction of improvements.

DEVISE –

A transfer of real property under a will.

DISCOUNT POINTS –

An added loan fee charged by a lender to make the yield on a lower-than-market-interest VA or FHA loan competitive with higher interest conventional loans.

DUE ON SALE CLAUSE –

A form of acceleration clause found in some mortgages, especially savings and loan mortgages, requiring the mortgagor to pay off the mortgage debt when selling the secured property, thus resulting in automatic maturity of the note at the lender's option.

E

EASEMENT –

A property interest which one person has in land owned by another entitling the holder of the interest to limited use or enjoyment of the other's land.

EMINENT DOMAIN –

The right of government, both state and federal, to take private property for a necessary public use, with just compensation paid to the owner.

ENCROACHMENT –

An unauthorized invasion or intrusion of a fixture or other real property wholly or partly upon another's property, thus reducing the size and value of the invaded property.

ENCUMBRANCE –

Any claim, lien, charge or liability attached to and binding upon real property which may lessen the value of the property but won't necessarily prevent transfer of title.

ENVIRONMENTAL IMPACT STATEMENT –

A report which includes a detailed description of a proposed development project with emphasis on the existing environment setting, viewed from both a local and regional perspective, and a discussion of the probable impact of the project on the environment during all phases.

EQUITY –

That interest or value remaining in property after payment of all liens or other charges on the property. An owner's equity is normally the monetary interest over and above the mortgage indebtedness.

ESCROW –

The process by which money and/or documents are held by a disinterested third person (a "stakeholder") until the satisfaction of the terms and conditions of the escrow instructions (as prepared by the parties to the escrow).

EXTENSION –

An agreement to continue the period of performance beyond the specified period.

F

FAIR MARKET VALUE –

The highest monetary price which a property would bring, if offered for sale for a reasonable period of time in a competitive market, to a seller who is willing but not compelled to sell, from a buyer, willing but not compelled to buy, both parties being fully informed of all the purposes to which the property is best adapted and is capable of being used.

FEASIBILITY STUDY –

An analysis of a proposed project with emphasis on the attainable income, probable expenses, and most advantageous use and design.

FEDERAL TAX LIEN –

A federal lien that attaches to real property, either if the federal estate tax is not paid, or if the taxpayer has violated the federal income tax or payroll tax laws.

FEE SIMPLE –

The largest estate one can possess in real property. A fee simple estate is the least limited interest and the most complete and absolute ownership in land: It is of indefinite duration, freely transferable, and inheritable. Fee simple title is sometimes referred to as "the fee."

FINANCE FEE –
A mortgage brokerage fee to cover the expenses incurred in placing the mortgage with a lending institution; a mortgage service charge or origination fee.

FINANCIAL STATEMENT –
A formal statement of the financial status and net worth of a person or company, setting forth and classifying assets and liabilities as of a specified date.

FIRST REFUSAL, RIGHT OF –
The right of a person to have the first opportunity either to purchase or lease real property.

FORBEARANCE –
A temporary suspension of mortgage payments agreed to by both lender and owner in times of financial difficulty. The

lender is actually delaying, or forbearing, starting foreclosure proceedings on the property while the owner catches up on payments.

FORECLOSURE –

The process whereby a lender, such as a bank, seeks to repossess a property where the owner has failed to comply with the terms of the mortgage or promissory note, such as not making a payment. Once the property has been foreclosed, the bank can then sell the house, using the money to pay its costs.

FREE AND CLEAR TITLE –

Title to real property which is absolute and unencumbered by any liens, mortgages, clouds, or other encumbrances.

FUNCTIONAL OBSOLESCENCE –

A loss in value of an improvement due to functional inadequacies, often caused by age or poor design.

G

GENERAL CONTRACTOR –

A construction specialist who enters into a formal construction contract with a land owner or master lessee to construct a real estate building or project.

GRANDFATHER CLAUSE –
Common expression used to convey the idea that something which was once permissible continues to be permissible despite changes in the controlling law.

GRANTEE –
The person who receives from the grantor a grant of real property.

GRANTOR –
The person transferring title to, or an interest in, real property. A grantor must be competent to convey;

GROSS AREA –
The total floor area of a building measured from the exterior of the walls (excluding those unenclosed).

GROSS INCOME MULTIPLIER –
A useful rule of thumb to estimate market value of in-

come-producing residential property. The multiplier is derived by using comparable sales divided by the actual or estimated monthly rentals and arriving at an acceptable average.

H

HIGH RISE –
A popular expression for a condominium or apartment building generally higher than six stories.

HIGHEST AND BEST USE –
That use which, at the time of appraising the property, is most likely to produce the greatest net return to the land and/or the building over a given period of time.

HOME EQUITY LINE OF CREDIT (HELOC) –
A revolving line of credit where the lender agrees to make available a certain amount of money for a certain time period secured by the value of the borrower's home. The funds are not advanced up front, but rather the borrower can choose when to use the money, much like a credit card. HELOCs are frequently used for major remodeling projects, to pay for

college tuition, or other large expenses. Generally the interest rate in HELOCs is adjustable.

HOME EQUITY LOAN –
Also known as a second mortgage, a personal loan secured by the value of the borrower's home. The money is transferred to the borrower up front and interest begins to accrue immediately.

HOMEOWNERS INSURANCE –
Insurance coverage is designed to protect a home and its contents, as well as shield the owner from liability for accidents and such on the property.

I

IMPROVED LAND –
Real property whose value has been enhanced by the addition of on-site and off-site improvements, such as roads, sewers, utilities, buildings, etc.; as distinguished from raw land.

IMPROVEMENTS –

Valuable additions made to property, amounting to more than repairs, costing labor and capital and intended to enhance the value of the property. Improvements of land would include grading, sidewalks, sewers, streets, utilities, etc. Improvements on land would include buildings, fences, and the like.

INCOME APPROACH –

An approach to the valuation or appraisal of real property as determined by the amount of net income the property will produce over its remaining economic life.

INCOME PROPERTY –

Property purchased primarily for the income to be derived plus certain tax benefits, such as accelerated depreciation. Income property can be commercial, industrial, or residential.

INSPECTION –

A visit to and review of the premises. A prudent purchaser of property always inspects the premises before closing.

INTEREST –

The sum paid or accrued in return for the use of money.

J

JUDGMENT LIEN –

A lien binding on all the real estate of a judgment-debtor and giving the holder of the judgment a right to levy (i.e. to seize) the land for satisfaction of the judgment.

JUDICIAL FORECLOSURE –

A method of foreclosing upon real property by means of a court supervised sale. After an appraisal, the court determines an upset price below which no bids to purchase will be accepted.

L

LAND CONTRACT –

Another name for an installment purchase contract, by which the buyer obtains equitable title (the right to use the property) while the seller retains legal title (recorded title) as security for payment of the balance of the purchase price.

LAND DESCRIPTION –

A description of a particular piece of real property.

LAND TRUST –

An association organized by common owners of real property, which holds title to the real property in the name of one or more trustees for the benefit of the owners, whose beneficial interests may be represented by trust certificates.

LANDLOCKED –

Real property having no access to a public road or way.

LEGAL DESCRIPTION –

A description that's complete enough that an independent surveyor could locate and identify a specific piece of real property.

LEGAL NOTICE –

That notice that's either implied or required by law. Constructive notice under the recording laws is also referred to as legal notice.

LETTER OF INTENT –

An expression of intent to invest, develop, or purchase without creating any firm legal obligation to do so.

LEVEL PAYMENT MORTGAGE –

A mortgage that's scheduled to be repaid in equal periodic payments that include both principal and interest.

LIEN –

A charge or claim which one person has upon the property of another as security for a debt or obligation. Liens can be created by agreement of the parties (mortgage) or by operation of law (tax liens).

LINE OF CREDIT –

A maximum amount of money a bank will lend one of its more reliable and credit worthy customers without need for any formal loan submission.

LOAN MODIFICATION –

A process in which mortgage loan terms are adjusted to lower monthly payments for homeowners at risk of foreclosure. Adjustments can include lowering interest rates, lengthening the term, or reducing the principle owed.

LOAN-TO-VALUE RATIO –

The ratio that the amount of the loan bears to the appraised value of the property or the sales price, whichever is lower.

M

MAINTENANCE –

The care and work put into a building to keep it in operation and productive use; the general repair and upkeep of a building. If maintenance is deferred, the building will suffer a loss in value.

MARKET VALUE –

The highest price, estimated in terms of money, which a property will bring if exposed for sale in the open market, allowing a reasonable time to find a purchaser who buys with knowledge of all the uses to which the property is adapted and for which it is capable of being used.

MARKETABLE TITLE –
Good or clear title reasonably free from risk of litigation over possible defects; also referred to as merchantable title. Marketable title need not, however, be perfect title.

MASTER PLAN –
A comprehensive plan to guide the long-term physical development of a particular area.

MECHANIC'S LIEN –
A statutory lien created in favor of materialmen and mechanics to secure payment for materials supplied and services rendered in the improvement, repair, or maintenance of real property.

MINERAL RIGHTS –
Rights to subsurface land and profits. Normally, when real property is conveyed, the grantee receives all right and title to the land, including everything above and below the surface,

unless excepted by the grantor.

MORTGAGE –

A legal document used to secure the performance of an obligation. In effect, the mortgage states that the lender can look to the property in the event the borrower defaults in payment of the note.

MORTGAGEE –

The one who receives and holds a mortgage as security for a debt; the lender; a lender or creditor who holds a mortgage as security for payment of an obligation.

MORTGAGOR –

The one who gives a mortgage as security for a debt; the borrower; usually the landowner; the borrower or debtor who hypothecates or puts up his property as security for an obligation.

N

NEGATIVE CASH FLOW –

The investment situation in which cash expenditures to maintain an investment (taxes, mortgage payments, maintenance, etc.) exceed the cash income received from the investment.

NEGOTIATION –

The transaction of business aimed at reaching a meeting of minds among the parties; bargaining.

NONCONFORMING USE –

A permitted use that was lawfully established and maintained but which no longer conforms to the current use regulations because of a change in the zoning.

O

OFFER –

A promise by one party to act or perform in a specified manner provided the other party will act or perform in the manner requested.

OPERATING EXPENSES –

Those periodic and necessary expenses that are essential to the continuous operation and maintenance of a property.

ORIGINATION FEE –

The finance fee charged by a lender for placing a mortgage, which covers initial costs such as preparation of documents and credit, inspection, and appraisal fees.

OVERIMPROVEMENT –

An improvement which by reason of excess size or cost isn't the highest and best use for the site on which it's placed.

P

PARCEL –

A specific portion of a larger tract; a lot.

PARTIAL RELEASE –

A clause found in a mortgage that directs the mortgagee to release certain parcels from the lien of the blanket mortgage upon the payment of a certain sum of money.

PERCOLATION TEST –

A hydraulic engineer's test of soil to determine the ability of the ground to absorb and drain water.

PLANNED UNIT DEVELOPMENT (PUD) –

A modern concept in housing designed to produce a high density of dwellings and maximum use of open spaces.

PLAT –

A map of a town, section, or subdivision indicating the location and boundaries of individual properties.

POINTS –

A generic term for a percentage of the principal loan amount which the lender charges for making the loan; each point is equal to 1% of the loan amount.

POWER OF ATTORNEY –

A written instrument authorizing a person (the attorney-in-fact) to act as the agent on behalf of another to the extent indicated in the instrument.

PREPAYMENT PENALTY –

The amount set by the creditor as a penalty to the debtor for paying off the debt before its maturity. The prepayment penalty is charged by the lender to recoup a portion of interest that he had planned to earn when he made the loan.

PRIVATE MORTGAGE INSURANCE –

A special form of insurance designed to permit lenders to increase their loan-to-market-value ratio, often up to 95 percent of the market value of the property.

PROCURING CAUSE –

That effort which brings about the desired result, as in producing the buyer for the listed property.

PROMISSORY NOTE –

An unconditional written promise of one person to pay a certain sum of money to another, or order, or bearer, at a future specified time.

PROPERTY –

The rights or interests a person has in the thing owned; not, in the technical sense, the thing itself. These rights include the right to possess, to use, to encumber, to transfer, and to exclude, commonly called the "bundle of rights."

PUNCH LIST –
A discrepancy list showing defects in construction that need some corrective work to bring the building up to standards set by the plans and specifications.

Q

QUITCLAIM DEED –
A deed of conveyance that operates, in effect, as a release of whatever interest the grantor has in the property; sometimes called a release deed.

R

RAW LAND –
Unimproved land; land in its unused natural state before the construction of improvements such as streets, lighting, sewers, and the like.

REAL ESTATE –

The physical land and appurtenances, including any structures; for all practical purposes synonymous with real property.

REAL PROPERTY –

All land and appurtenances to land, including buildings, structures, fixtures, fences, and improvements erected upon or affixed to the same; excluding, however, growing crops.

RECORDING –

The act of entering into the book of public records the written instruments affecting the title to real property, such as deeds, mortgages, contracts of sale, options, assignments, and the like. Proper recordation imparts constructive notice to all the world of the existence of the recorded document and its contents.

REFINANCE –

The act of obtaining a new loan to pay off an existing loan; the process of paying off one loan with the proceeds from another.

REPRODUCTION COST –

The cost, on the basis of current prices, of reproducing a new replica property with the same or fairly similar material.

RESTRICTIONS –

Limitations on the use of property. Private restrictions are created by means of restrictive covenants written into real property instruments, such as deeds and leases.

RESTRICTIVE COVENANT –

A private agreement, usually contained in a deed, which restricts the use and occupancy of real property.

REVERSE MORTGAGE –

A special type of home loan available to seniors that converts a portion of the equity in a home into cash. Unlike a traditional home equity loan or second mortgage, no repayment is required until the borrower(s) no longer use the home as their principal residence.

RIGHT-OF-WAY –

The right or privilege, acquired through accepted usage or by contract, to pass over a designated portion of the property of another.

S

SALE AND LEASEBACK –

A transaction in which, typically, an owner sells his improved property and as part of the same transaction signs a long-term lease and remains in possession.

SETBACK –

Zoning restrictions on the amount of land required surrounding improvements; the amount of space required between the lot line and the building line.

SHORT SALE –

In real estate, a sale of a property by a lender where the sale price is less than is what is owed on the mortgage.

SPECIAL ASSESSMENT –

A tax or levy customarily imposed against only those specific parcels of realty that will benefit from a proposed public improvement, as opposed to a general tax on the entire community.

SPECIAL WARRANTY DEED –

A deed in which the grantor warrants or guarantees the title only against defects arising during the period of his tenure and ownership of the property and not against defects existing before the time of his ownership.

SURVEY –

The process by which boundaries are measured and land areas are determined; the on-site measurement of lot lines, dimensions, and position of houses in a lot including the determination of any existing encroachments or easements.

SURVIVORSHIP –

The right of survivorship is that special feature of a joint tenancy whereby all title, right and interest of a decedent joint tenant in certain property passes to the surviving joint tenants by operation of law, free from claims of heirs and creditors of the decedent.

T

TAX LIEN –
A general statutory lien imposed against real property for failure to pay taxes. There are federal tax liens and state tax liens.

TITLE INSURANCE –
A comprehensive contract of indemnity under which the title company agrees to reimburse the insured for any loss if title isn't as represented in the policy.

TITLE SEARCH –
An examination of the public records to determine what, if any, defects there are in the chain of title.

TRUST DEED –
A real property security device (also called a deed of trust) very similar to a mortgage, except that there are three parties, the trustor, the trustee, and the beneficiary (the lender).z]

TRUST FUND ACCOUNT –

An account set up by a broker at a bank or other recognized depository, into which the broker deposits all funds entrusted to him by his principal or others.

TURNKEY PROJECT –

A development term meaning the complete construction package from groundbreaking to the completion of the building. All that's left undone is to turn over the keys to the buyer.

U

UPSET PRICE –

A minimum price set by a court in a judicial foreclosure, below which the property may not be sold by a court appointed commissioner at public auction; the minimum price which can be accepted for the property after the court has had the property appraised.

USURY –

Charging a rate of interest in excess of that permitted by law.

V

VARIANCE –

Permission obtained from governmental zoning authorities to build a structure or conduct a use that's expressly prohibited by the current zoning laws; an exception from the zoning laws.

W

WARRANTY –

A guaranty by the seller, covering the title as well as the physical condition of
the property.

WARRANTY DEED –

A deed in which the grantor fully warrants good clear title to the premises. Also called a general warranty deed.

Y

YIELD –

The return on an investment or the amount of profit, stated as a percentage of the amount invested.

Z

ZONING –

The regulation of structures and uses of property within designated districts or zones. Zoning regulates and affects such things as use of the land, types of structure permitted, building heights, setbacks, and density (the ratio of land area to improvement area).

www.ingramcontent.com/pod-product-compliance
Lightning Source LLC
LaVergne TN
LVHW011209080426
835508LV00007B/687